POETRY FROM CRESCENT MOON

William Shakespeare: *The Sonnets*
edited, with an introduction by Mark Tuley

William Shakespeare: *Complete Poems*
edited and introduced by Mark Tuley

Shakespeare: Love, Poetry and Magic in Shakespeare's Sonnets and Plays
by B.D. Barnacle

Edmund Spenser: *Heavenly Love: Selected Poems*
selected and introduced by Teresa Page

Edmund Spenser: *Amoretti*
edited by Teresa Page

Robert Herrick: *Delight In Disorder: Selected Poems*
edited and introduced by M.K. Pace

Sir Thomas Wyatt: *Love For Love: Selected Poems*
selected and introduced by Louise Cooper

John Donne: *Air and Angels: Selected Poems*
selected and introduced by A.H. Ninham

D.H. Lawrence: *Being Alive: Selected Poems*
edited with an introduction by Margaret Elvy

D.H. Lawrence: Symbolic Landscapes
by Jane Foster

D.H. Lawrence: Infinite Sensual Violence
by M.K. Pace

Percy Bysshe Shelley: *Paradise of Golden Lights: Selected Poems*
selected and introduced by Charlotte Greene

Thomas Hardy: *Her Haunting Ground: Selected Poems*
edited, with an introduction by A.H. Ninham

Sexing Hardy: Thomas Hardy and Feminism
by Margaret Elvy

Emily Brontë: *Darkness and Glory: Selected Poems*
selected and introduced by Miriam Chalk

John Keats: *Bright Star: Selected Poems*
edited with an introduction by Miriam Chalk

John Keats: *Poems of 1820*
edited with an introduction by Miriam Chalk

Henry Vaughan: *A Great Ring of Pure and Endless Light: Selected Poems*
selected and introduced by A.H. Ninham

The Crescent Moon Book of Love Poetry
edited by Louise Cooper

The Crescent Moon Book of Mystical Poetry in English
edited by Carol Appleby

The Crescent Moon Book of Nature Poetry From Langland to Lawrence
edited by Margaret Elvy

The Crescent Moon Book of Metaphysical Poetry
edited and introduced by Charlotte Greene

The Crescent Moon Book of Elizabethan Love Poetry
edited and introduced by Carol Appleby

The Crescent Moon Book of Romantic Poetry
edited and introduced by L.M. Poole

Peter Redgrove: Here Comes the Flood
by Jeremy Mark Robinson

Sex-Magic-Poetry-Cornwall: A Flood of Poems
by Peter Redgrove, edited with an essay by Jeremy Mark Robinson

Brigitte's Blue Heart
by Jeremy Reed

Claudia Schiffer's Red Shoes
by Jeremy Reed

By-Blows: Uncollected Poems
by D.J. Enright

Petrarch, Dante and the Troubadours: The Religion of Love and Poetry
by Cassidy Hughes

Dante: *Selections From the Vita Nuova*
translated by Thomas Okey

Arthur Rimbaud: *Selected Poems*
edited and translated by Andrew Jary

Arthur Rimbaud: *A Season in Hell*
edited and translated by Andrew Jary

Rimbaud: Arthur Rimbaud and the Magic of Poetry
by Jeremy Mark Robinson

Friedrich Hölderlin: *Hölderlin's Songs of Light: Selected Poems*
translated by Michael Hamburger

Rainer Maria Rilke: *Dance the Orange:* Selected Poems
translated by Michael Hamburger

Rilke: Space, Essence and Angels in the Poetry of Rainer Maria Rilke
by B.D. Barnacle

German Romantic Poetry: Goethe, Novalis, Heine, Hölderlin
by Carol Appleby

Arseny Tarkovsky: *Life, Life: Selected Poems*
translated by Virginia Rounding

Emily Dickinson: *Wild Nights: Selected Poems*
selected and introduced by Miriam Chalk

Cavafy: Anatomy of a Soul
by Matt Crispin

Diana
by Henry Constable

Delia
by Samuel Daniel

Idea
by Michael Drayton

Astrophil and Stella
by Sir Philip Sidney

Elizabethan Sonnet Cycles
by Daniel, Drayton, Sidney, Spenser and Shakespeare

Darkness and Glory
Selected Poems

Darkness and Glory

Selected Poems

Emily Brontë

Edited by Miriam Chalk

CRESCENT MOON

CRESCENT MOON PUBLISHING
P.O. Box 1312, Maidstone
Kent, ME14 5XU
Great Britain, www.crmoon.com

First published 1996. Second edition 2008. Revised 2014/ 16.
Introduction © Miriam Chalk, 1996, 2008, 2014, 2016.

Printed and bound in the U.S.A.
Set in Garamond Book 12 on 18pt.
Designed by Radiance Graphics.

British Library Cataloguing in Publication data

Brontë, Emily, 1818-1848
Darkness and Glory: Selected Poems - 2nd ed. (British Poets Series)
I. Title II. Page, Teresa
821.8

ISBN 9781861711793
ISBN 9781861715326

Contents

Loud without the wind was roaring   13

High waving heather, 'neath stormy blasts bending
    17

That wind, I used to hear it swelling   18

The wind, I hear it sighing   19

Come, walk with me   20

And like myself lone, wholly lone   22

O wander not so far away!   23

A Farewell to Alexandria   25

Lines by Claudia   27

Alone I sat; the summer day   29

May flowers are opening   31

To the bluebell   33

Fair sinks the summer evening now   34

Fall, leaves, fall; die, flowers, away   36

Shall Earth no more inspire thee   37

All hushed and still within the house   39

I'm happiest when most away   40

All day I've toiled, but not with pain   41

How still, how happy! Those are words   43

Ah! why, because the dazzling sun   45

To Imagination   48

How clear she shines! How quietly   50

O between distress and pleasure   52

Mild the mist upon the hill   54

'Tis moonlight, summer moonlight   55

The starry night shall tidings bring   56

The night is darkening round me   57

Sleep brings no joy to me   58

O Dream, where art thou now   60

The Philosopher   61

Stanzas   64

Spellbound   66

No coward soul is mine   67

Remembrance   69

Song   71

Anticipation   73

A Day Dream   76

Death   80

Honour's Martyr   82

Stanzas   86

Illustrations   87

A Note On Emily Brontë   93

The Brontë sisters, by their brother Bramwell, c. 1834

"Loud without the wind was roaring"

Loud without the wind was roaring
Through the waned autumnal sky;
Drenching wet, the cold rain pouring
Spoke of stormy winters nigh.

All too like that dreary eve
Sighed within repining grief;
Sighed at first, but sighed not long –
Sweet – How softly sweet it came!
Wild words of an ancient song,
Undefined, without a name.

"It was spring, for the skylark was singing."
Those words, they awakened a spell –
They unlocked a deep fountain whose springing
Nor Absence nor Distance can quell.

In the gloom of a cloudy November,
They uttered the music of May;
They kindled the perishing ember
Into fervour that could not decay.

Awaken on all my dear moorlands
The wind in its glory and pride!
O call me from valleys and highlands
To walk by the hill-river's side!

It is swelled with the first snowy weather;
The rocks they are icy and hoar
And darker waves round the long heather
And the fern-leaves are sunny no more,

There are no yellow-stars on the mountain,
The blue-bells have long died away
From the brink of the moss-bedded fountain,
From the side of the wintery brae –

But lovelier than corn-fields allow having
In emerald and scarlet and gold
Are the slopes where the north-wind is raving,
And the glens where I wandered of old.

"It was morning; the bright sun was beaming.'
How sweetly that brought back to me
The time when nor labour nor dreaming
Broke the sleep of the happy and the free.

But blindly we rose as the dusk heaven
Was melting to amber and blue;

And swift were the wings to our feet given
While we traversed the meadows of dew.

For the moors, for the moors where the short grass
Like velvet beneath us should lie!
For the moors, for the moors where each high pass
Rose sunny against the clear sky!

For the moors where the linnet was trilling
Its song on the old granite stone;
Where the lark – the wild skylark was filling
Every breast with delight like its own.

What language can utter the feeling
That rose when, in exile afar,
On the brow of a lonely hill kneeling
I saw the brown heath growing there.

It was scattered and stunted, and told me
That soon even that would be gone;
Its whispered, "The grim walls enfold me;
I have bloomed in my last summer's sun."

But not the loved music whose waking
Makes the soul of the Swiss die away
Has a spell more adored and heart-breaking
Than in its half blighted bells lay.

The spirit that bent 'neath its power,
How it longed, how it burned to be free!
If I could have wept in that hour
Those tears had been heaven to me.

Well, well, the sad minutes are moving
Though loaded with trouble and pain;
And sometime the loved and the loving
Shall meet on the mountains again.

"High waving heather, 'neath stormy blasts bending"

High waving heather, 'neath stormy blasts bending,
Midnight and moonlight and bright shining stars;
Darkness and glory rejoicingly blending,
Earth rising to heaven and heaven descending,
Man's spirit away from its drear dungeon sending,
Bursting the fetters and breaking the bars.

All down the mountain sides, wild forests lending
One might voice to the life-giving wind;
Rivers their banks in the jubilee rending,
Fast through the valleys a reckless course wending,
Wider and deeper their waters extending,
Leaving a desolate desert behind.

Shining and lowering and swelling and dying,
Changing for ever from midnight to noon;
Roaring like thunder, like soft music sighing,
Shadows on shadows advancing and flying,
Lightning-bright flashes the deep gloom defying,
Coming as swiftly and fading as soon.

"That wind, I used to hear it swelling"

That wind, I used to hear it swelling
With joy divinely deep;
You might have seen my hot tears welling,
But rapture made me weep.

I used to love on winter nights
To lie and dream alone
Of all the rare and real delights
My early years had known;

And oh, above the rest of those
That coming time should bear,
Like heaven's own glorious stars they rose
Still beaming bright and fair.

"The wind, I hear it sighing"

The wind, I hear it sighing
With Autumn's saddest sound;
Withered leaves as thick are lying
As spring-flowers on the ground –

This dark night has won me
To wander far away –
Old feelings gather fast upon me
Like vultures round their prey.

Kind were they once, and cherished
But cold and cheerless now –
I would their lingering shades had perished
When their light left my brow.

"Come, walk with me"

Come, walk with me;
There's only thee
To bless my spirit now;
We used to love on winter nights
To wander through the snow.
Can we not woo back old delights?
The clouds rush dark and wild;
They fleck with shade our mountain heights
The same as long ago,
And on the horizon at last
In looming masses piled;
While moonbeams flash and fly so fast
We scarce can say they smiled.

Come, walk with me – come, walk with me;
We were not once so few;
But Death has stolen our company
As sunshine steals the dew:
He took them one by one, and we
Are left, the only two;
So closer would my feelings twine,
Because they have no stay but thine.

"Nay, call me not; it may not be;
Is human love so true?
Can Friendship's flower droop on for years
And then revive anew?
No; though the soil be wet with tears,
How fair soe'er it grew;
The vital sap once perished
Will never flow again;
And surer than that dwelling dread,
The narrow dungeon of the dead,
Time parts the hearts of men."

"And like myself lone, wholly lone"

And like myself lone, wholly lone,
It seems the day's long sunshine glow;
And like myself it makes its moan
In unexpected woe.

Give we the hills our equal prayer:
Earth's breezy hills and heaven's blue sea;
We ask for nothing further here
But our own hearts and liberty.

Ah! could my hand unlock its chain,
How gladly would I watch it soar,
And ne'er regret and ne'er complain
To see its shining eyes no more.

But let me think that if today
It pines in cold captivity,
Tomorrow both shall soar away,
Eternally, entirely Free.

"O wander not so far away!"

O wander not so far away!
O love, forgive this selfish tear.
It may be sad for thee to stay
But how can I live lonely here?

The still May morn is warm and bright,
Young flowers look fresh and grass is green,
And in the haze of glorious light
Our long low hills are scarcely seen.

The woods – even now their small leaves hides
The blackbird and the stockdove well
And high in heaven so blue and wide
A thousand strains of music swell.

He looks on all with eyes that speak
So deep, so drear a woe to me!
There is a faint red on his cheek
Not like the bloom I used to see.

Call Death – yes, Death, he is thine own!
The grave must close those limbs around
And hush, for ever hush the tone

I lived above all earthly sound.

Well, pass away with the other flowers,
Too dark for them, too dark for thee
Are the hours to come, the joyless hours
That Time is treasuring up for me –

If thou hast sinned in this world of care
'Twas but the dust of thy drear abode –
Thy soul was pure when it entered here
And pure it will go again to God!

A Farewell to Alexandria

I've seen this dell in July's shine
As lovely as an angel's dream;
Above, heaven's depth of blue divine:
Around, the evening's golden beam –

I've seen the purple heather-bell
Look out by many a storm-worn stone
And oh, I've known such music swell,
Such wild notes wake these passes lone –

So soft, yet so intensely felt –
So low, yet so distinctly heard
My breath would pause, my eyes would melt
And my tears dew the green heath-sward –

I'd linger here a summer day
Nor care how fast the hours flew by
Nor mark the sun's departing ray
Smile sadly glorious from the sky

Then, then I might have laid thee down
And deemed thy sleep would gentle be
I might have left thee, darling one

And thought thy God was guarding thee!

But now, there is no wandering glow
No gleam to say that God is nigh:
And coldly spreads thy couch of snow
And harshly sounds thy lullaby.

Forests of heather dark and long
Wave their brown branching arms above
And they must soothe thee with their song
And they must shield my child of love!

Alas the flakes are heavily falling
They cover fast each guardian crest:
And chilly white their shroud is palling
Thy frozen limbs and freezing breast –

Wakes up the storm more madly wild
The mountain drifts are tossed on high –
Farewell unblessed, unfriended child,
I cannot bear to watch thee die!

Lines by Claudia

I did not sleep 'twas noon of day
I saw the burning sunshine fall.
The long grass bending where I lay
The blue sky brooding over all

I heard the mellow hum of bees
And singing birds and sighing trees
And far away in woody dell
The music of the Sabbath bell

I did not dream remembrance still
Clasped round my heart its fetters chill
But I am sure the soul is free
To leave its clay a little while
Or how in exile misery
Could I have seen my country smile

In English fields my limbs were laid
With English turf beneath my head
My spirit wandered o'er that shore
Where nought but it may wander more
Yet if the soul can thus return
I nccd not and I will not mourn

And vainly did you drive me far
With leagues of ocean stretched between
My mortal flesh you might debar
But not the eternal fire within

My Monarch died to rule forever
A heart that can forget him never
And dear to me aye doubly dear
Though shut within the silent tomb
His name shall be for whom I bear
This long sustained and hopeless doom

And brighter in the hour of woe
Than in the blaze of victory's pride
That glory shedding star shall glow
For which we fought and bled and died.

"Alone I sat; the summer day"

Alone I sat; the summer day
Had died in smiling light away;
I saw it die, I watched it fade
From misty hill and breezeless glade;

And thoughts in my soul were rushing,
And my heart bowed beneath their power;
And tears within my eyes were gushing
Because I could not speak the feeling,
The solemn joy around me stealing
In that divine, untroubled hour.

I asked myself, "O why has heaven
Denied the precious gift to me,
The glorious gift to many given
To speak their thoughts in poetry?

"Dreams have encircled me," I said,
"From careless childhood's sunny time;
Visions by ardent fancy fed
Since life was in its morning prime."
But now, when I had hoped to sing,
My fingers strike a tuneless string;

And still the burden of the strain
Is "Strive no more; 'tis all in vain."

"May flowers are opening"

May flowers are opening
And leaves unfolding free;
There are bees in every blossom
And birds on every tree.

The sun is gladly shining,
The stream sings merrily,
And I only am pining
And all is dark to me.

O – cold, cold is my heart;
It will not, cannot rise;
It feels no sympathy
With those refulgent skies.

Dead, dead is my joy,
I long to be at rest;
I wish the damp earth covered
This desolate breast.

If I were quite alone
It might not be so drear;
When all hope was gone

At least I could not fear.

But the glad eyes around me
Must weep as mine have done
And I must see the same gloom
Eclipse their morning sun.

If heaven would rain on me
That future storm of care
So their fond hearts were free
I'd be content to bear.

Alas, as lightning withers
The young and aged tree,
Both they and I shall fall beneath
The fate we cannot flee.

To the Bluebell

Sacred watcher, wave thy bells!
Fair hill flower and woodland child!
Dear to me in deep green dells –
Dearest on the mountains wild.

Bluebell, even as all divine
I have seen my darling shine –
Bluebell, even as wan and frail
I have seen my darling fail –
Thou hast found a voice for me,
And soothing words are breathed by thee.

Thus they murmur, "Summer's sun
Warms me till my life is done.
Would I rather choose to die
Under winter's ruthless sky?

"Glad I bloom and calm I fade;
Weeping twilight dews my bed;
Mourner, mourner, dry thy tears –
Sorrow comes with lengthened years!"

"Fair sinks the summer evening now"

Fair sinks the summer evening now
In softened glory round my home;
The sky upon its holy brow
Wears not a cloud that speaks of gloom.

The old tower, shrined in golden light,
Looks down on the descending sun –
So gently evening blends with night
You scarce can say that day is done –

And this is just the joyous hour
When we were wont to burst away,
To 'scape from labour's tyrant power
And cheerfully go out to play.

Then why is all so sad and lone?
No merry footstep on the stair –
No laugh – no heart-awaking tone,
But voiceless silence everywhere.

I've wandered round our garden-ground
And still it seemed at every turn
That I should greet approaching feet

And words upon the breezes borne.

In vain – they will not come today
And morning's beam will rise as drear;
Then tell me – are they gone for aye
Our sun-blinks through the mists of care?

Ah no, reproving Hope doth say
Departed joys 'tis fond to mourn
When every storm that hides their ray
Prepares a more divine return.

"Fall, leaves, fall; die, flowers, away"

Fall, leaves, fall; die, flowers, away;
Lengthen night and shorten day;
Every leaf speaks bliss to me
Fluttering from the autumn tree,
I shall smile when wreaths of snow
Blossom where the rose should grow;
I shall sing when night's decay
Ushers in a drearier day.

"Shall earth no more inspire thee"

Shall Earth no more inspire thee,
Thou lonely dreamer now?
Since passion may not fire thee
Shall nature cease to bow?

Thy mind is ever moving
In regions dark to thee;
Recall its useless roving –
Come back and dwell with me.

I know my mountain breezes
Enchant and soothe thee still –
I know my sunshine pleases
Despite thy wayward will.

When day with evening blending
Sinks from the summer sky,
I've seen thy spirit bending
In fond idolatry.

I've watched thee every hour;
I know my mighty sway,
I know my magic power

To drive thy griefs away.

Few hearts to mortals given
On earth so wildly pine;
Yet none would ask a Heaven
More like this Earth than thine.

Then let my winds caress thee;
Thy comrade let me be –
Since nought beside can less thee,?
Return and dwell with me.

"All hushed and still within the house"

All hushed and still within the house;
Without – all wind and driving rain;
But something whispers to my mind,
Through rain and through the wailing wind,
　　Never again.
Never again? Why not again?
Memory has power as real as thine.

"I'm happiest when most away"

I'm happiest when most away
I can bear my soul from its home of clay
On a windy night when the moon is bright
And the eye can wander through worlds of light –

When I am not and none beside –
Nor earth nor sea nor cloudless sky –
But only spirit wandering wide
Through infinite immensity.

"All day I've toiled, but not without pain"

All day I've toiled, but not with pain,
In learning's golden mine;
And now at eventide again
The moonbeams softly shine.

There is no snow upon the ground,
No frost on wind or wave;
The south wind blew with gentlest sound
And broke their icy grave.

'Tis sweet to wander here at night
To watch the winter die,
With heart as summer sunshine light
And warm as summer sky.

O may I never lose the peace
That lulls me gently now,
Though time should change my youthful face,
And years should shade my brow!

True to myself, and true to all.
May I be healthful still,

And turn away from passion's call,
And curb my own wild will.

"How still, how happy! Those are words"

How still, how happy! Those are words
That once would scarce agree together;
I loved the splashing of the surge,
The changing heaven, the breezy weather,

More than smooth seas and cloudless skies
And solemn, soothing, softened airs
That in the forest woke no sighs
And from the green spray shook no tears.

How still, how happy! Now I feel
Where silence dwells is sweeter far
Than laughing mirth's most joyous swell
However pure its raptures are.

Come, sit down on this sunny stone:
'Tis wintry light o'er flowerless moors –
But sit – for we are all alone
And clear expand heaven's breathless shores.

I could think in the withered grass
Spring's budding wreaths we might discern;
The violet's eye might shyly flash

And young leaves shoot among the fern.

It is but thought – full many a night
The show shall clothe those hills afar
And storms shall add a drearier blight
And winds shall wage a wilder war,

Before the lark may herald in
Fresh foliage twined with blossoms fair
And summer days again begin
Their glory-haloed crown to wear.

Yet my heart loves December's smile
As much as July's golden beam;
Then let us sit and watch the while
The blue ice curdling on the stream.

"Ah! why, because the dazzling sun"

Ah! why, because the dazzling sun
Restored my earth to joy
Have you departed, every one,
And left a desert sky?

All through the night, your glorious eyes
Were gazing down in mine,
And with a full heart's thankful sighs
I blessed that watch divine!

I was at peace, and drank your beams
As they were life to me
And revelled in my changeful dreams
Like petrel on the sea.

Thought followed thought – star followed star
Through boundless regions on,
While one sweet influence, near and far,
Thrilled through and proved us one.

Why did the morning rise to break
So great, so pure a spell,
And scorch with fire the tranquil cheek

Where your cool radiance fell?

Blood-red he rose, and arrow-straight
His fierce beams struck my brow:
The soul of Nature sprang elate,
But mine sank sad and low!

My lids closed down – yet through their veil
I saw him blazing still;
And bathe in gold the misty dale,
And flash upon the hill.

I turned me to the pillow then
To call back Night, and see
Your worlds of solemn light, again
Throb with my heart and me!

It would not do – the pillow glowed
And glowed both roof and floor,
And birds sang loudly in the wood,
And fresh winds shook the door.

The curtain waved, the wakened flies
Were murmuring round my room,
Imprisoned there, till I should rise
And give them leave to roam.

O Stars and Dreams and Gentle Night;
O Night and Stars return!
And hide me from the hostile light
That does not warm, but burn –

That drains the blood of suffering men;
Drinks tears, instead of dew;
Let me sleep through his blinding reign,
And only wake with you!

To Imagination

When weary with the long day's care,
And earthly change from pain to pain,
And lost, and ready to despair,
Thy kind voice calls me back again –
O my true friend, I am not lone
While thou canst speak with such a tone!

So hopeless is the world without,
The world within I doubly prize;
Thy world where guile and hate and doubt
And cold suspicion never rise;
Where thou and I and Liberty
Have undisputed sovereignty.

What matters is that all around
Danger and grief and darkness lie,
If but within our bosom's bound
We hold a bright unsullied sky,
Warm with ten thousand mingled rays
Of suns that know no winter days?

Reason indeed may oft complain
For Nature's sad reality,

And tell the suffering heart how vain
Its cherished dreams must always be;
And Truth may rudely trample down
The flowers of Fancy newly blown.

But thou art ever there to bring
The hovering visions back and breake
New glories o'er the blighted spring
And call a lovelier life from death,
And whisper with a voice divine
Of real worlds as bright as thine.

I trust not to thy phantom bliss,
Yet still in evening's quiet hour
With never-failing thankfulness
I welcome thee, benignant power,
Sure solacer of human cares
And brighter hope when hope despairs.

"How clear she shines! How quietly"

How clear she shines! How quietly
I lie beneath her silver light
While Heaven and Earth are whispering me,
"To-morrow wake, but dream tonight."

Yes, Fancy, come, my Fairy love!
These throbbing temples, softly kiss;
And bend my lonely couch above
And bring me rest and bring me bliss.

The world is going – Dark world, adieu!
Grim world, go hide thee till the day;
The heart thou canst not all subdue
Must still resist if thou delay!

Thy love I will not, will not share;
Thy hatred only wakes a smile;
Thy grief may wound – thy wrong may tear,
But, oh, thy lies shall ne'er beguile!

While gazing on the stars that glow
Above me in that stormless sea,
I long to hope that all the woe

Creation knows, is held in thee!

And this shall be my dream tonight –
I'll think the heaven of glorious spheres
Is rolling on its course of light
In endless bliss through endless years;

I'll think there's not one world above,
Far as these straining eyes can see,
Where Wisdom ever laughed at Love,
Or Virtue crouched to Infamy;

Where, writhing 'neath the strokes of Fate,
The mangled wretch was forced to smile;
To match his patience 'gainst her hate,
His heart rebellious all the while;

Where Pleasure still will lead to wrong,
And helpless Reason warn in vain;
And Truth is weak and Treachery strong,
And Joy the shortest path to Pain;

And Peace, the lethargy of grief;
And Hope, a phantom of the soul;
And Life, a labour void and brief;
And Death, the despot of the whole!

"O between distress and pleasure"

O between distress and pleasure
Fond affection cannot be;
Wretched hearts in vain would treasure
Friendship's joys when others flee.

Well I know thine eye would never
Smile, while mine grieved, willingly;
Yet I know thine eye for ever
Could not weep in sympathy.

Let us part, the time is over
When I thought and felt like thee;
I will be an Ocean rover,
I will sail the desert sea.

Isles there are beyond its billow:
Lands where woe may wander free;
And, beloved, thy midnight pillow
Will be soft unwatched by me.

Not on each returning morrow
When thy heart bounds ardently
Need'st thou then dissemble sorrow,

Marking my despondency.

Day by day some dreary token
Will forsake thy memory
Till at last all old links broken
I shall be a dream to thee.

"Mild the mist upon the hill"

Mild the mist upon the hill,
Telling not of stones tomorrow;
No; the day has wept its fill,
Spent its store of silent sorrow.

Oh, I'm gone back to the days of youth,
I am a child once more;
And 'neath my father's sheltering roof,
And near the old hall door,

I watch this cloudy evening fall,
After a day of rain:
Blue mists, sweet mists of summer pall
The horizon's mountain-chain.

The damp stands in the long, green grass
As thick as morning's tears;
And dreamy scents of fragrance pass
That breathe of other years.

"'Tis moonlight, summer moonlight"

'Tis moonlight, summer moonlight,
All soft and still and fair;
The solemn hour of midnight
Breathes sweet thoughts everywhere,

But most where trees are sending
Their breezy boughs on high,
Or stooping low are lending
A shelter from the sky.

And there in those wild bowers
A lovely form is laid;
Green grass and dew-steeped flowers
Wave gently round her head.

"The starry night shall tidings bring"

"The starry night shall tidings bring:
Go out upon the breezy moor,
Watch for a bird with sable wing
And beak and talons dropping gore.

Look not around, look not beneath,
But mutely trace its airy way;
Mark where it lights upon the heath
Then, wanderer, kneel thee down and pray.

What future may await thee there
I will not and I dare not tell,
But Heaven is moved by fervent prayer
And God is mercy - fare thee well!"

"The night is darkening round me"

The night is darkening round me,
The wild winds coldly blow;
But a tyrant spell has bound me
And I cannot, cannot go.

The giant trees are bending
Their bare boughs weighed with snow,
And the storm is fast descending
And yet I cannot go.

Clouds beyond clouds above me,
Wastes beyond wastes below;
But nothing drear can move me;
I will not, cannot go.

"Sleep brings no joy to me"

Sleep brings no joy to me,
Remembrance never dies;
My soul is given to misery
And lives in sighs.

Sleep brings no rest to me;
The shadows of the dead
My waking eyes may never see
Surround my bed.

Sleep brings no hope to me;
In soundest sleep they come,
And with their doleful imagery
Deepen the gloom.

Sleep brings no strength to me,
No power renewed to brave,
I only sail a wilder sea,
A darker wave.

Sleep brings no friend to me
To soothe and aid to bear;
They all gaze, oh, how scornfully,

And I despair.

Sleep brings no wish to knit
My harnessed heart beneath;
My only wish is to forget
In sleep of death.

"O Dream, where are thou now?"

O Dream, where art thou now?
Long years have past away
Since last from off thine angel brow
I saw the light decay.

Alas, alas for me
Thou wert so bright and fair,
I could not think thy memory
Would yield me nought but air!

The sun-beam and the storm,
The summer-eve divine,
The silent night of solemn calm,
The full moon's cloudless shine,

Were entwined with thee,
But now with weary pain,
Lost vision! 'tis enough for me –
Thou canst not sing again.

The Philosopher

"Enough of thought, philosopher!
Too long hast thou been dreaming
Unlightened, in this chamber drear,
While summer's sun is beaming!
Space - sweeping soul, what sad refrain
Concludes thy musings once again?

"Oh, for the time when I shall sleep
Without identity,
And never care how rain may steep,
Or snow may cover me!
No promised heaven, these wild desires,
Could all, or half fulfil;
No threatened hell, with quenchless fires,
Subdue this quenchless will!"

"So said I, and still say the same;
Still, to my death, will say -
Three gods, within this little frame,
Are warring night and day;
Heaven could not hold them all, and yet
They all are held in me;
And must be mine till I forget

My present entity!
Oh, for the time, when in my breast
Their struggles will be o'er!
Oh, for the day, when I shall rest,
And never suffer more!"

"I saw a spirit, standing, man,
Where thou dost stand – an hour ago,
And round his feet three rivers ran,
Of equal depth, and equal flow –
"A golden stream – and one like blood;
And one like sapphire, seemed to be;
But, where they joined their triple flood
It tumbled in an inky sea.

The spirit sent his dazzling gaze
Down through that ocean's gloomy night
Then, kindling all, with sudden blaze,
The glad deep sparkled wide and bright –
White as the sun, far, far more fair
Than its divided sources were!"

"And even for that spirit, seer,
I've watched and sought my life – time long;
Sought him in heaven, hell, earth and air –
An endless search, and always wrong!
Had I but seen his glorious eye

Once light the clouds that wilder me,
I ne'er had raised this coward cry
To cease to think and cease to be;
I ne'er had called oblivion blest,
Nor, stretching eager hands to death,
Implored to change for senseless rest
This sentient soul, this living breath –
Oh, let me die – that power and will
Their cruel strife may close;
And conquered good, and conquering ill
Be lost in one repose!"

Stanzas

Often rebuked, yet always back returning
To those first feelings that were born with me,
And leaving busy chase of wealth and learning
For idle dreams of things that cannot be:

To-day, I will seek not the shadowy region;
Its unsustaining vastness waxes drear;
And visions rising, legion after legion,
Bring the unreal world too strangely near.

I'll walk, but not in old heroic traces,
And not in paths of high morality,
And not among the half-distinguished faces,
The clouded forms of long-past history.

I'll walk where my own nature would be leading:
It vexes me to choose another guide:
Where the gray flocks in ferny glens are feeding;
Where the wild wind blows on the mountain side.

What have those lonely mountains worth revealing?
More glory and more grief than I can tell:

The earth that wakes one human heart to feeling
Can centre both the worlds of Heaven and Hell.

Spellbound

The night is darkening round me,
The wild winds coldly blow;
But a tyrant spell has bound me
And I cannot, cannot go.

The giant trees are bending
Their bare boughs weighed with snow.
And the storm is fast descending,
And yet I cannot go.

Clouds beyond clouds above me,
Wastes beyond wastes below;
But nothing dear can move me;
I will not, cannot go.

"No coward soul is mine"

No coward soul is mine,
No trembler in the world's storm-troubled sphere:
I see Heaven's glories shine,
And faith shines equal, arming me from fear.

O God within my breast,
Almighty, ever-present Deity!
Life – that in me has rest,
As I – undying Life – have power in Thee!

Vain are the thousand creeds
That move men's hearts: unutterably vain;
Worthless as withered weeds,
Or idlest froth amid the boundless main,

To waken doubt in one
Holding so fast by Thine infinity;
So surely anchored on
The steadfast rock of immortality.

With wide-embracing love
Thy spirit animates eternal years,
Pervades and broods above,

Changes, sustains, dissolves, creates, and tears.

Though earth and man were gone,
And suns and universes ceased to be,
And Thou were left alone,
Every existence would exist in Thee.

There is not room for Death,
Nor atom that his might could render void:
Thou – THOU art Being and Breath,
And what THOU art may never be destroyed.

Remembrance

Cold in the earth – and the deep snow piled above thee,
Far, far, removed, cold in the dreary grave!
Have I forgot, my only Love, to love thee,
Severed at last by Time's all-severing wave?

Now, when alone, do my thoughts no longer hover
Over the mountains, on that northern shore,
Resting their wings where heath and fern-leaves cover
Thy noble heart for ever, ever more?

Cold in the earth – and fifteen wild Decembers,
From those brown hills, have melted into spring:
Faithful, indeed, is the spirit that remembers
After such years of change and suffering!

Sweet Love of youth, forgive, if I forget thee,
While the world's tide is bearing me along;
Other desires and other hopes beset me,
Hopes which obscure, but cannot do thee wrong!

No later light has lightened up my heaven,
No second morn has ever shone for me;
All my life's bliss from thy dear life was given,

All my life's bliss is in the grave with thee.

But, when the days of golden dreams had perished,
And even Despair was powerless to destroy;
Then did I learn how existence could be cherished,
Strengthened, and fed without the aid of joy.

Then did I check the tears of useless passion –
Weaned my young soul from yearning after thine;
Sternly denied its burning wish to hasten
Down to that tomb already more than mine.

And, even yet, I dare not let it languish,
Dare not indulge in memory's rapturous pain;
Once drinking deep of that divinest anguish,
How could I seek the empty world again?

Song

The linnet in the rocky dells,
  The moor-lark in the air,
The bee among the heather bells
  That hide my lady fair:

The wild deer browse above her breast;
  The wild birds raise their brood;
And they, her smiles of love caressed,
  Have left her solitude!

I ween, that when the grave's dark wall
  Did first her form retain,
They thought their hearts could ne'er recall
  The light of joy again.

They thought the tide of grief would flow
  Unchecked through future years;
But where is all their anguish now,
  And where are all their tears?

Well, let them fight for honour's breath,
  Or pleasure's shade pursue –
The dweller in the land of death

Is changed and careless too.

And, if their eyes should watch and weep
  Till sorrow's source were dry,
She would not, in her tranquil sleep,
  Return a single sigh!

Blow, west-wind, by the lonely mound,
  And murmur, summer-streams –
There is no need of other sound
  To soothe my lady's dreams.

Anticipation

How beautiful the earth is still,
To thee – how full of happiness?
How little fraught with real ill,
Or unreal phantoms of distress!
How spring can bring thee glory, yet,
And summer win thee to forget
December's sullen time!
Why dost thou hold the treasure fast,
Of youth's delight, when youth is past,
And thou art near thy prime?

When those who were thy own compeers,
Equals in fortune and in years,
Have seen their morning melt in tears,
To clouded, smileless day;
Blest, had they died untried and young,
Before their hearts went wandering wrong, –
Poor slaves, subdued by passions strong,
A weak and helpless prey!

'Because, I hoped while they enjoyed,
And by fulfilment, hope destroyed;
As children hope, with trustful breast,

I waited bliss – and cherished rest.
A thoughtful spirit taught me soon,
That we must long till life be done;
That every phase of earthly joy
Must always fade, and always cloy:

'This I foresaw – and would not chase
The fleeting treacheries;
But, with firm foot and tranquil face,
Held backward from that tempting race,
Gazed o'er the sands the waves efface,
To the enduring seas –
There cast my anchor of desire
Deep in unknown eternity;
Nor ever let my spirit tire,
With looking for WHAT IS TO BE!

"It is hope's spell that glorifies,
Like youth, to my maturer eyes,
All Nature's million mysteries,
The fearful and the fair –
Hope soothes me in the griefs I know;
She lulls my pain for others' woe,
And makes me strong to undergo
What I am born to bear.

Glad comforter! will I not brave,

Unawed, the darkness of the grave?
Nay, smile to hear Death's billows rave –
Sustained, my guide, by thee?
The more unjust seems present fate,
The more my spirit swells elate,
Strong, in thy strength, to anticipate
Rewarding destiny!

A Day Dream

On a sunny brae alone I lay
One summer afternoon;
It was the marriage-time of May,
With her young lover, June.

From her mother's heart seemed loath to part
That queen of bridal charms,
But her father smiled on the fairest child
He ever held in his arms.

The trees did wave their plumy crests,
The glad birds carolled clear;
And I, of all the wedding guests,
Was only sullen there!

There was not one, but wished to shun
My aspect void of cheer;
The very gray rocks, looking on,
Asked, "What do you here?"

And I could utter no reply;
In sooth, I did not know
Why I had brought a clouded eye

To greet the general glow.

So, resting on a heathy bank,
I took my heart to me;
And we together sadly sank
Into a reverie.

We thought, "When winter comes again,
Where will these bright things be?
All vanished, like a vision vain,
An unreal mockery!

"The birds that now so blithely sing,
Through deserts, frozen dry,
Poor spectres of the perished spring,
In famished troops will fly.

"And why should we be glad at all?
The leaf is hardly green,
Before a token of its fall
Is on the surface seen!"

Now, whether it were really so,
I never could be sure;
But as in fit of peevish woe,
I stretched me on the moor,

A thousand thousand gleaming fires
Seemed kindling in the air;
A thousand thousand silvery lyres
Resounded far and near:

Methought, the very breath I breathed
Was full of sparks divine,
And all my heather-couch was wreathed
By that celestial shine!

And, while the wide earth echoing rung
To that strange minstrelsy
The little glittering spirits sung,
Or seemed to sing, to me:

"O mortal! mortal! let them die;
Let time and tears destroy,
That we may overflow the sky
With universal joy!

"Let grief distract the sufferer's breast,
And night obscure his way;
They hasten him to endless rest,
And everlasting day.

"To thee the world is like a tomb,
A desert's naked shore;

To us, in unimagined bloom,
It brightens more and more!

"And, could we lift the veil, and give
One brief glimpse to thine eye,
Thou wouldst rejoice for those that live,
BECAUSE they live to die."

The music ceased; the noonday dream,
Like dream of night, withdrew;
But Fancy, still, will sometimes deem
Her fond creation true.

Death

Death! that struck when I was most confiding.
In my certain faith of joy to be –
Strike again, Time's withered branch dividing
From the fresh root of Eternity!

Leaves, upon Time's branch, were growing brightly,
Full of sap, and full of silver dew;
Birds beneath its shelter gathered nightly;
Daily round its flowers the wild bees flew.

Sorrow passed, and plucked the golden blossom;
Guilt stripped off the foliage in its pride
But, within its parent's kindly bosom,
Flowed for ever Life's restoring tide.

Little mourned I for the parted gladness,
For the vacant nest and silent song –
Hope was there, and laughed me out of sadness;
Whispering, "Winter will not linger long!"

And, behold! with tenfold increase blessing,
Spring adorned the beauty-burdened spray;
Wind and rain and fervent heat, caressing,

Lavished glory on that second May!

High it rose – no winged grief could sweep it;
Sin was scared to distance with its shine;
Love, and its own life, had power to keep it
From all wrong – from every blight but thine!

Cruel Death! The young leaves droop and languish;
Evening's gentle air may still restore –
No! the morning sunshine mocks my anguish-
Time, for me, must never blossom more!

Strike it down, that other boughs may flourish
Where that perished sapling used to be;
Thus, at least, its mouldering corpse will nourish
That from which it sprung – Eternity.

Honour's Martyr

The moon is full this winter night;
The stars are clear, though few;
And every window glistens bright
With leaves of frozen dew.

The sweet moon through your lattice gleams,
And lights your room like day;
And there you pass, in happy dreams,
The peaceful hours away!

While I, with effort hardly quelling
The anguish in my breast,
Wander about the silent dwelling,
And cannot think of rest.

The old clock in the gloomy hall
Ticks on, from hour to hour;
And every time its measured call
Seems lingering slow and slower:

And, oh, how slow that keen-eyed star
Has tracked the chilly gray!
What, watching yet! how very far

The morning lies away!

Without your chamber door I stand;
Love, are you slumbering still?
My cold heart, underneath my hand,
Has almost ceased to thrill.

Bleak, bleak the east wind sobs and sighs,
And drowns the turret bell,
Whose sad note, undistinguished, dies
Unheard, like my farewell!

To-morrow, Scorn will blight my name,
And Hate will trample me,
Will load me with a coward's shame –
A traitor's perjury.

False friends will launch their covert sneers;
True friends will wish me dead;
And I shall cause the bitterest tears
That you have ever shed.

The dark deeds of my outlawed race
Will then like virtues shine;
And men will pardon their disgrace,
Beside the guilt of mine.

For, who forgives the accursed crime
Of dastard treachery?
Rebellion, in its chosen time,
May Freedom's champion be;

Revenge may stain a righteous sword,
It may be just to slay;
But, traitor, traitor, – from THAT word
All true breasts shrink away!

Oh, I would give my heart to death,
To keep my honour fair;
Yet, I'll not give my inward faith
My honour's NAME to spare!

Not even to keep your priceless love,
Dare I, Beloved, deceive;
This treason should the future prove,
Then, only then, believe!

I know the path I ought to go
I follow fearlessly,
Inquiring not what deeper woe
Stern duty stores for me.

So foes pursue, and cold allies
Mistrust me, every one:

Let me be false in others' eyes,
If faithful in my own.

Stanzas

I'll not weep that thou art going to leave me,
There's nothing lovely here;
And doubly will the dark world grieve me,
While thy heart suffers there.

I'll not weep, because the summer's glory
Must always end in gloom;
And, follow out the happiest story -
It closes with a tomb!

And I am weary of the anguish
Increasing winters bear;
Weary to watch the spirit languish
Through years of dead despair.

So, if a tear, when thou art dying,
Should haply fall from me,
It is but that my soul is sighing,
To go and rest with thee.

Illustrations

Including images of Emily Brontë.

Editions of Wuthering Heights

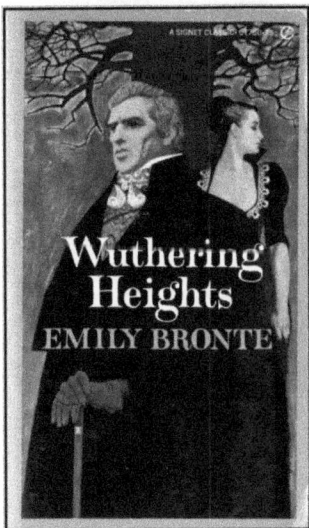

Wuthering Heights (1939)

A Note On Emily Brontë

by Miriam Chalk

EMILY BRONTE (1818-48) as a poet is still neglected today. Her novel, *Wuthering Heights*, however, remains one of the great English novels. It continues to sell, continues to be adapted for radio, theatre, film and television, continues to inspire readers and be cited by critics. *Wuthering Heights* has entered British culture as both a serious work in academic circles and a series of cliches in popular culture. For scholars, *Wuthering Heights* is a superbly crafted and atmospheric piece of fiction which takes its place beside the great works of the 19th century (*Tess of the d'Urbervilles, Middlemarch, Great Expectations, Pride and Prejudice*).

For feminists, Emily Brontë has been appropriated as a proto-feminist, working largely in isolation in patriarchal Yorkshire, away from the metropolitan centres of culture, yet producing fiery fiction and poetry.[1] For the general reader, *Wuthering Heights* is a fabulously moody, passionate and romantic book, with a powerful sense of pace, fully rounded characters and a thrill of mystery about it. It is one of those 'classic novels' that one can periodically return to and enjoy each time. It repays many rereadings, like the novels by Dickens, Hardy, Austen and Eliot cited above. *Wuthering Heights* is also, like those novels, a set text for educational courses. One of the things that sets *Wuthering Heights* apart from other novels is the intensity of the sexual desire evoked in it. It is this erotic intensity that gives the novel its grandeur and power. The same thing happens with Shakespeare's tragedies – the greater the desire, the more there seems to be at stake. The level of erotic desire in *Wuthering Heights* raises the novel from being a melodrama (tending towards soap opera) and a 'great' tragic novel. Emily Brontë knows her craft well, even though *Wuthering Heights* is her only novel or lengthy work. She knows, for example, the primary rule of all romantic fiction: the lovers must be kept apart, so that the feelings increase and are kept on the boil. If Cathy and Heathcliff were allowed to have each other totally, with

---

1 '*Wuthering Heights* is a powerful novel of female desire. One could set the novel in a tradition of French feminist *écriture feminine*, it's a powerful expression of 'women's writing'. The women characters are empowered – they write and speak, they are the subjects (not the objects) of discourse, they challenge the prevailing (patriarchal) ideology. (Regina Barreca: "The Power of Excommunication: Sex and the Feminine Text in *Wuthering Heights*", in Barreca, ed: *Sex and Death in Victorian Literature*, Macmillan 1990, 229)

nothing stopping their togetherness, there would be no tensions, no agony, no drama, in short. One way or another, they are kept apart. Another surprising thing is that the mad, passionate Cathy only appears in half the novel - the rest deals with the second generation characters. Yet it is the passion of Cathy and Heathcliff that is so memorable, that is the central feature of the book. The imagery - of Cathy and Heathcliff meeting on the wild Yorkshire moors - has endured over a hundred and fifty years and more. From time to time this imagery turns up in popular culture (Monty Python famously spoofed the novel and had Cathy and Heathcliff communicating by semaphore). Emily Brontë certainly conjured up the wildness of the moors, making them a vivid parallel to Cathy's wild behaviour. The wind whistling through the heather in Winter is indeed the atmosphere of the novel, and also of her poetry. In poem after poem we find loving evocations of the moors: we hear of 'the breezy moor' (in "The starry night shall tidings bring"), the 'flowerless moors' (in "How still, how happy! Those are words"), and of 'the moors where the linnet was trilling/ Its song on the old granite stone' (in "Loud without the wind was roaring", the most powerful of Brontë's moor-poems). The key element of the moors is the expanse of sky and the wind that rages across it: the wind is without doubt Brontë's favourite element, and is the sound that accompanies the clichéd adaptions of *Wuthering Heights*. In the poetry we hear of 'The wind in its glory and pride!' ("Loud without the wind was roaring"), 'the life-giving wind' ("High waving heather, 'neath stormy blasts bending"), 'That wind, I used to hear it swelling/ With joy divinely deep' ("That wind, I used to hear it swelling"), 'the wailing wind' ("All hushed and still within the house"), 'And winds shall wage a wilder war' ("How still, how happy!"), 'The wild winds coldly blow' ("The night is darkening round me"). These simple, elemental facts – the heather, the moor, the wind, the night – are what recur in Brontë's poems, time after time. Dells, snow, linnets, rocky crags, greyness, darkness, graves; one can practically see her composing her lines as she sits in a darkened house at night, with the wind whistling outside. This is a clichéd image, again, of the artist at work (the Northern European artist, from Dante through Shakespeare to the Brothers Grimm and Paul Claudel). Yet this is very much how poets create, absorbing their surroundings. Many of Emily Brontë's poems concern the characters and events of the world she invented with her sisters, the 'Gondal' poems. Yet even in this imagined world the imagery and sensuality of the bare, elemental moors shines through. Half of Brontë's poems may reside in some invented world, in some mental Gondal, but they are actually centred on a passionately desirous person living in relative solitude in provincial England. The words which crop up again and again in Brontë's poems, after the elemental terms 'wind', 'heather', 'night', 'flowers', and 'evening', are 'alone', 'solitude' and 'lonely'. Like the Cathy persona, Brontë's poetic persona is someone who yearns for larger, wilder, more colourful things, even as she loves the sights and sounds of her homeland.

The typical Brontë poem opens with an evocation of a summer of love, the age-old binding together of the delights and flowers and sunshine of Spring and Summer with the blossoming of heterosexual love or some earlier, happier time. As the poem progressed, it darkens, day becomes evening or night, Summer becomes Winter, love fades and solitude becomes the norm. So many Brontë poems open relatively summery or bright and darken as the poem progresses: "The blue bell is the sweetest flower", "In the same place, where Nature wore", "The linnet in the rocky dells", 'A Farewell to Alexandria', and 'To the bluebell'. However these poems begin, Brontë's poetic persona cannot help but bring in loneliness, sorrow, graves and death. The progression always seems to be towards some sort of lonely melancholy, a reflective reverie in which the poet muses on her past. We see the same tendency in Thomas Hardy's poems (there are many parallels between Hardy and Brontë, not only in their poetry).

One must not over-emphasize the apparently pessimistic or death-conscious aspect of Emily Brontë's poetry. There is lightness, too.

> How do I love on summer nights
> To sit within this Norman door
> ("How do I love on summer nights")

> Bluebell, even as all divine
> I have seen my darling shine
> ('To the blue bell')

> How beautiful the Earth is still
> To thee, how full of Happiness
> ("How beautiful the Earth is still")

> Child of Delight! with sunbright hair,

And seablue, seadeep eyes
Spirit of Bliss...
("Heavy hangs the raindrop")

There's no doubt that much of Emily Brontë's poetry concerns decline, loss, decay and death, a withering away; yet this is always countered by a vivacious and sometimes overpowering love of life, a yearning for peace and happiness. What comes across in Brontë's poetry, apart from its intense sensual and elemental qualities, it is the strength of the will to live, the indomitability of the poetic persona's spirit.

Beauties, Beasts, and Enchantment

CLASSIC FRENCH FAIRY TALES

Translated and with an Introduction
by Jack Zipes

A collection of 36 classic French fairy tales translated by renowned writer Jack Zipes.
Cinderella, Beauty and the Beast, Sleeping Beauty and *Little Red Riding Hood* are among the classic fairy tales in this amazing book.
Includes illustrations from fairy tale collections.
Jack Zipes has written and published widely on fairy tales.

'Terrific... a succulent array of 17th and 18th century 'salon' fairy tales'
- *The New York Times Book Review*

'These tales are adventurous, thrilling in a way fairy tales are meant to be... The translation from the French is modern, happily free of archaic and hyperbolic language... a fine and sophisticated collection' - *New York Tribune*

'Enjoyable to read... a unique collection of French regional folklore' - *Library Journal*

'Charming stories accompanied by attractive pen-and-ink drawings' - *Chattanooga Times*

Introduction and illustrations   612pp.   ISBN 9781861712510 Pbk   ISBN 9781861713193 Hbk

MAURICE SENDAK

& the art of children's book illustration

L.M. Poole

Maurice Sendak is the widely acclaimed American children's book author and illustrator. This critical study focuses on his famous trilogy, *Where the Wild Things Are*, *In the Night Kitchen* and *Outside Over There*, as well as the early works and Sendak's superb depictions of the Grimm Brothers' fairy tales in *The Juniper Tree*. L.M. Poole begins with a chapter on children's book illustration, in particular the treatment of fairy tales. Sendak's work is situated within the history of children's book illustration, and he is compared with many contemporary authors.

Fully illustrated. The book has been revised and updated for this edition.

ISBN 9781861714282 Pbk   ISBN 9781861713469 Hbk

Life, Life
Selected Poems

Arseny Tarkovsky

translated and edited by Virginia Rounding

Arseny Tarkovsky is the neglected Russian poet, father of the acclaimed film director
Andrei Tarkovsky. This new book gathers together many of Tarkovsky's most lyrical
and heartfelt poems, in Rounding's clear, new translations. Many of Tarkovsky's poems
appeared in his son's films, such as *Mirror, Stalker, Nostalghia* and *The Sacrifice*.
There is an introduction by Rounding, and a bibliography of both Arseny and
Andrei Tarkovsky.

Bibliography and notes 124pp 3rd ed ISBN 9781861712660 Hbk ISBN 9781861711144

In the Dim Void

Samuel Beckett's Late Trilogy:
Company, Ill Seen, Ill Said and *Worstward Ho*

by Gregory Johns

This book discusses the luminous beauty and dense, rigorous poetry of Samuel Beckett's late works, *Company, Ill Seen, Ill Said* and *Worstward Ho*. Gregory Johns looks back over Beckett's long writing career, charting the development from the *Molloy-Malone Dies-Unnamable* trilogy through the 'fizzles' of the 1960s to the elegiac lyricism of the *Company* series. Johns compares the trilogy with late plays such as *Ghosts, Footfalls* and *Rockaby*.

Bibliography, notes. Illustrated. 120pp
ISBN 9781861712974 Pbk and ISBN 9781861712608 Hbk
9781861713407 E-book

CRESCENT MOON PUBLISHING

web: www.crmoon.com e-mail: cresmopub@yahoo.co.uk

ARTS, PAINTING, SCULPTURE

The Art of Andy Goldsworthy
Andy Goldsworthy: Touching Nature
Andy Goldsworthy in Close-Up
Andy Goldsworthy: Pocket Guide
Andy Goldsworthy In America
Land Art: A Complete Guide
The Art of Richard Long
Richard Long: Pocket Guide
Land Art In the UK
Land Art in Close-Up
Land Art In the U.S.A.
Land Art: Pocket Guide
Installation Art in Close-Up
Minimal Art and Artists In the 1960s and After
Colourfield Painting
Land Art DVD, TV documentary
Andy Goldsworthy DVD, TV documentary
The Erotic Object: Sexuality in Sculpture From Prehistory to the Present Day
Sex in Art: Pornography and Pleasure in Painting and Sculpture
Postwar Art
Sacred Gardens: The Garden in Myth, Religion and Art
Glorification: Religious Abstraction in Renaissance and 20th Century Art
Early Netherlandish Painting
Leonardo da Vinci
Piero della Francesca
Giovanni Bellini
Fra Angelico: Art and Religion in the Renaissance
Mark Rothko: The Art of Transcendence
Frank Stella: American Abstract Artist
Jasper Johns
Brice Marden
Alison Wilding: The Embrace of Sculpture
Vincent van Gogh: Visionary Landscapes
Eric Gill: Nuptials of God
Constantin Brancusi: Sculpting the Essence of Things
Max Beckmann
Caravaggio
Gustave Moreau
Egon Schiele: Sex and Death In Purple Stockings
Delizioso Fotografico Fervore: Works In Process 1
Sacro Cuore: Works In Process 2
The Light Eternal: J.M.W. Turner
The Madonna Glorified: Karen Arthurs

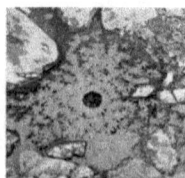

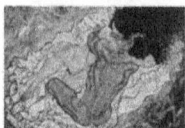

LITERATURE

J.R.R. Tolkien: The Books, The Films, The Whole Cultural Phenomenon
J.R.R. Tolkien: Pocket Guide
Tolkien's Heroic Quest
The *Earthsea* Books of Ursula Le Guin
Beauties, Beasts and Enchantment: Classic French Fairy Tales
German Popular Stories by the Brothers Grimm
Philip Pullman and *His Dark Materials*
Sexing Hardy: Thomas Hardy and Feminism
Thomas Hardy's *Tess of the d'Urbervilles*
Thomas Hardy's *Jude the Obscure*
Thomas Hardy: The Tragic Novels
Love and Tragedy: Thomas Hardy
The Poetry of Landscape in Hardy
Wessex Revisited: Thomas Hardy and John Cowper Powys
Wolfgang Iser: Essays and Interviews
Petrarch, Dante and the Troubadours
Maurice Sendak and the Art of Children's Book Illustration
Andrea Dworkin
Cixous, Irigaray, Kristeva: The *Jouissance* of French Feminism
Julia Kristeva: Art, Love, Melancholy, Philosophy, Semiotics and Psychoanalysis
Hélène Cixous I Love You: The *Jouissance* of Writing
Luce Irigaray: Lips, Kissing, and the Politics of Sexual Difference
Peter Redgrove: Here Comes the Flood
Peter Redgrove: Sex-Magic-Poetry-Cornwall
Lawrence Durrell: Between Love and Death, East and West
Love, Culture & Poetry: Lawrence Durrell
Cavafy: Anatomy of a Soul
German Romantic Poetry: Goethe, Novalis, Heine, Hölderlin
Feminism and Shakespeare
Shakespeare: Love, Poetry & Magic
The Passion of D.H. Lawrence
D.H. Lawrence: Symbolic Landscapes
D.H. Lawrence: Infinite Sensual Violence
Rimbaud: Arthur Rimbaud and the Magic of Poetry
The Ecstasies of John Cowper Powys
Sensualism and Mythology: The Wessex Novels of John Cowper Powys
Amorous Life: John Cowper Powys and the Manifestation of Affectivity (H.W. Fawkner)
Postmodern Powys: New Essays on John Cowper Powys (Joe Boulter)
Rethinking Powys: Critical Essays on John Cowper Powys
Paul Bowles & Bernardo Bertolucci
Rainer Maria Rilke
Joseph Conrad: *Heart of Darkness*
In the Dim Void: Samuel Beckett
Samuel Beckett Goes into the Silence
André Gide: Fiction and Fervour
Jackie Collins and the Blockbuster Novel
Blinded By Her Light: The Love-Poetry of Robert Graves
The Passion of Colours: Travels In Mediterranean Lands
Poetic Forms

POETRY

Ursula Le Guin: Walking In Cornwall
Peter Redgrove: Here Comes The Flood
Peter Redgrove: Sex-Magic-Poetry-Cornwall
Dante: Selections From the Vita Nuova
Petrarch, Dante and the Troubadours
William Shakespeare: Sonnets
William Shakespeare: Complete Poems
Blinded By Her Light: The Love-Poetry of Robert Graves
Emily Dickinson: Selected Poems
Emily Brontë: Poems
Thomas Hardy: Selected Poems
Percy Bysshe Shelley: Poems
John Keats: Selected Poems
Joh n Keats: Poems of 1820
D.H. Lawrence: Selected Poems
Edmund Spenser: Poems
Edmund Spenser: Amoretti
John Donne: Poems
Henry Vaughan: Poems
Sir Thomas Wyatt: Poems
Robert Herrick: Selected Poems
Rilke: Space, Essence and Angels in the Poetry of Rainer Maria Rilke
Rainer Maria Rilke: Selected Poems
Friedrich Hölderlin: Selected Poems
Arseny Tarkovsky: Selected Poems
Arthur Rimbaud: Selected Poems
Arthur Rimbaud: A Season in Hell
Arthur Rimbaud and the Magic of Poetry
Novalis: Hymns To the Night
German Romantic Poetry
Paul Verlaine: Selected Poems
Elizaethan Sonnet Cycles
D.J. Enright: By-Blows
Jeremy Reed: Brigitte's Blue Heart
Jeremy Reed: Claudia Schiffer's Red Shoes
Gorgeous Little Orpheus
Radiance: New Poems
Crescent Moon Book of Nature Poetry
Crescent Moon Book of Love Poetry
Crescent Moon Book of Mystical Poetry
Crescent Moon Book of Elizabethan Love Poetry
Crescent Moon Book of Metaphysical Poetry
Crescent Moon Book of Romantic Poetry
Pagan America: New American Poetry

MEDIA, CINEMA, FEMINISM and CULTURAL STUDIES

J.R.R. Tolkien: The Books, The Films, The Whole Cultural Phenomenon
J.R.R. Tolkien: Pocket Guide
The *Lord of the Rings* Movies: Pocket Guide
The Cinema of Hayao Miyazaki
Hayao Miyazaki: *Princess Mononoke*: Pocket Movie Guide
Hayao Miyazaki: *Spirited Away*: Pocket Movie Guide
Tim Burton : Hallowe'en For Hollywood
Ken Russell
Ken Russell: *Tommy*: Pocket Movie Guide
The Ghost Dance: The Origins of Religion
The Peyote Cult
Cixous, Irigaray, Kristeva: The *Jouissance* of French Feminism
Julia Kristeva: Art, Love, Melancholy, Philosophy, Semiotics and Psychoanalysis
Luce Irigaray: Lips, Kissing, and the Politics of Sexual Difference
Hélene Cixous I Love You: The *Jouissance* of Writing
Andrea Dworkin
'Cosmo Woman': The World of Women's Magazines
Women in Pop Music
HomeGround: The Kate Bush Anthology
Discovering the Goddess (Geoffrey Ashe)
The Poetry of Cinema
The Sacred Cinema of Andrei Tarkovsky
Andrei Tarkovsky: Pocket Guide
Andrei Tarkovsky: *Mirror*: Pocket Movie Guide
Andrei Tarkovsky: *The Sacrifice*: Pocket Movie Guide
Walerian Borowczyk: Cinema of Erotic Dreams
Jean-Luc Godard: The Passion of Cinema
Jean-Luc Godard: *Hail Mary*: Pocket Movie Guide
Jean-Luc Godard: *Contempt*: Pocket Movie Guide
Jean-Luc Godard: *Pierrot le Fou*: Pocket Movie Guide
John Hughes and Eighties Cinema
Ferris Bueller's Day Off: Pocket Movie Guide
Jean-Luc Godard: Pocket Guide
The Cinema of Richard Linklater
Liv Tyler: Star In Ascendance
Blade Runner and the Films of Philip K. Dick
Paul Bowles and Bernardo Bertolucci
Media Hell: Radio, TV and the Press
An Open Letter to the BBC
Detonation Britain: Nuclear War in the UK
Feminism and Shakespeare
Wild Zones: Pornography, Art and Feminism
Sex in Art: Pornography and Pleasure in Painting and Sculpture
Sexing Hardy: Thomas Hardy and Feminism

The Light Eternal is a model monograph, an exemplary job. The subject matter of the book is beautifully
organised and dead on beam. (Lawrence Durrell)
It is amazing for me to see my work treated with such passion and respect. (Andrea Dworkin)

CRESCENT MOON PUBLISHING
P.O. Box 1312, Maidstone, Kent, ME14 5XU, Great Britain. www.crmoon.com

cresmopub@yahoo.co.uk   www.crescentmoon.org.uk